Succeeding in the
SECONDARY CLASSROOM

This book is dedicated to my maternal grandparents and their daughter, Rebecca.

Succeeding in the
SECONDARY CLASSROOM

Strategies
for Middle
and High School
Teachers

Harriett Arnold

CORWIN PRESS, INC.
A Sage Publications Company
2455 Teller Road
Thousand Oaks, CA 91320-2218
E-mail: order@corwinpress.com
Call: 805-499-9774 Fax: 800-4-1-SCHOOL
www.corwinpress.com

For information:

 Corwin Press, Inc.
A Sage Publications Company
2455 Teller Road
Thousand Oaks, California 91320
E-mail: order@corwinpress.com

Sage Publications Ltd.
6 Bonhill Street
London EC2A 4PU
United Kingdom

Sage Publications India Pvt. Ltd.
M-32 Market
Greater Kailash I
New Delhi 110 048 India

Printed in the United States of America

Library of Congress Cataloging-in-Publication Data

Arnold, Harriett.
   Succeeding in the secondary classroom: Strategies for middle and
high school teachers / by Harriett Arnold.
       p.   cm.
   Includes index.
   ISBN 0-8039-6794-2 (cloth: acid-free paper)
   ISBN 0-8039-6795-0 (pbk.: acid-free paper)
   1. High school teachers—United States.   2. High school teaching—
United States.   3. Middle school teachers—United States.   4. First year
teachers—United States.   I. Title.
   LB1777.2 .A75   2000
   373. 1102—dc21   00-01001

This book is printed on acid-free paper.

01   02   03   04   05   06   07   7   6   5   4   3   2   1

Corwin Editorial Assistant:	Julia Parnell
Production Editor:	Denise Santoyo
Editorial Assistant:	Candice Crosetti
Typesetter/Designer:	Lynn Miyata
Indexer:	Teri Greenberg
Cover Designer:	Michelle Lee

Contents

Preface

I am a teacher at heart, and there are moments in the classroom when I can hardly hold the joy. . . .

—Parker Palmer, *The Courage to Teach*

What This Book Is About

New teachers are being hired in middle and high school classrooms every day. The teaching journey begins during the preservice period in university classrooms throughout the country, and the journey continues with constant changes during the teaching career.

Succeeding in the Secondary Classroom: Strategies for Middle and High School Teachers offers useful teaching ideas for secondary beginning teachers who wish to focus on their students, parents, colleagues, teaching associates, and school site administrators. This book provides examples and directions that will be useful to beginning teachers in middle and high schools.

A secondary teacher is faced with myriad decisions during the first week and month of school. In addition to providing tools, techniques, and strategies that might be helpful during the first year of teaching, this book provides suggested forms, strategies, and teaching ideas to help with the adjustment. I realize that teaching in a middle or high school classroom is different; the secondary teacher will teach many students during the course of a five-period (or block) day.

This book is the culmination of researching and assembling materials from high school beginning teachers during the course of 3 years. Some of the materials were shared by master teachers in the process of working with beginning teachers in a public school district. The content of this book has its foundation in the teaching ideas and suggestions that I have collected from high school beginning teachers in selected San Francisco Bay Area high schools. The material in this book is practical, useful, and authentic. The strategies have been made in an effort to provide future high school beginning teachers with the knowledge already gained by teachers in the beginning teacher program.

This book sets the first year of teaching in a middle or high school in context and deals with concerns that are aimed primarily at the secondary teacher. It offers a practical, realistic, and organized approach for secondary beginning teachers.

A secondary teacher has a difficult job that is filled with lesson planning, classroom management, discipline, parents, administrators, and adolescents who have particular needs at all hours of the day. A beginning secondary teacher will find that life is filled with fantasy and awe and will be exhausting at the end of the first day, week, and month of school. This book will fill the void for the secondary teacher that has often been neglected in the literature.

With sometimes 200 students per day, the first days of school are utterly overwhelming; the first months of school are filled with uncertainty, problems, and pitfalls that can overpower the first-year teacher.

There are several publications that are focused directly on the elementary school teacher, but few of these publications target the beginning middle and high school teacher. This book is aimed at those secondary beginning teachers who are content-focused and currently teaching in interdisciplinary classrooms and who are also in need of strategies and activities that will be helpful to them on their teaching journey.

This book is not intended to be used exclusively but in cooperation with other materials in the classroom. A secondary teacher who is successful plans for the students in the classroom while keeping in mind the needs of all the students who will enter the class during the period of an academic year.

**This information should be used in your classroom
and examined for specific situations.**

Acknowledgments

Thanks to each of the beginning teachers, veteran teachers, and instructional vice principals who participated in this project. Thanks also to Michael who provided the vision, Marion who provided the guidance, and Sue who provided perseverance when many of the original members changed or moved on to greater opportunities. The genesis for this publication was made possible with a grant from the William and Flora Hewlett Foundation for secondary beginning teachers.

A special thanks to Alice, who never gave up on this book, and my husband, John, who continues to be a very patient man.

The contributions of the following reviewers are also gratefully acknowledged:

Jana Lane
Program Specialist, Stockton Unified School District
Stockton, California

Charles Ecklund
Director, Secondary Education, Conejo Unified School District
Thousand Oaks, California

About the Author

Harriett Arnold is Associate Professor and Director of the Single Subject Credential Programs in the Gladys L. Benerd School of Education at the University of the Pacific in Stockton, California. A veteran educator, she has served as an elementary school teacher, middle school vice-principal, elementary school principal, secondary administrator, director of personnel and staff development, and consultant. She serves as the Facilitator of the Network for Research on Affective Factors in Learning, a special interest group of educators interested in the role of emotions in learning, which is funded by the Association for Supervision and Curriculum Development. In addition, her teacher training projects have involved teacher training for the Ministry of Education in the Bahamas, where she trained elementary teachers in the area of reading. *Succeeding in the Secondary Classroom: Strategies for Middle and High School Teachers* is her second book.

Before the First Days of School

Congratulations! You have completed your student teaching and practicum in secondary education, and you now are ready for your first teaching job. Your family and friends have cheered you on and provided support for this new venture. There was much excitement in the air when you signed all of your school district paperwork, and it is now a reality: You are a teacher!

You are now an expert in your content area, adolescent behavior, curriculum and instruction, classroom management, educational foundations, theories, and philosophy. You will be in demand by students, parents, colleagues, and administrators and there will be several expectations of you from others as well as from yourself.

In your district, there will be many names, telephone numbers, and offices to remember. They are all important, so you will need to place this information in a central location. Every department will have paperwork that must be completed and returned quickly by you. As you attend meetings and read materials, take the time to write down telephone numbers, fax numbers, and e-mail addresses that you may need. This will save you time in the future.

**You are about to begin the first month of school,
and this time you will be the teacher.**

Thinking About Your First Teaching Job

♦ Arrange a visit to tour the building with others. This is also an opportunity to personally meet the custodians, secretaries, department chair, and teacher colleagues you will be working with.

♦ Acquaint yourself with and locate the teachers' lounge, adult restrooms, work rooms, supply closets, special classrooms, auditorium, computer labs, and gymnasium, and learn where your students hang out (see Form 1.1).

This first visit may also provide you with an early introduction to the politics of the school, your department, and the district.

Classroom Design

Do you have your own classroom? If so, you can create your own physical classroom to reflect your personality and content area. Using Form 1.2 as a guide, sit alone in your classroom and mentally plan your room.

School Policies

The first days of school on a middle or high school campus are filled with challenges and excitement. This is your first teaching job, and you have worked very hard to arrive at this place in your teaching journey.

You will soon learn that there are district and school policies that are important to the students as well as to the teachers (see Form 1.3). Some of these policies may seem unimportant to you, but pay attention to all of your district and school policies. They are important and significant to you as a teacher. By attending meetings, you may learn how each policy is important. Also, when an emergency arises in your classroom, it is best that you are familiar with these policies so that you are prepared for the situation.

FORM 1.1. Sample Checklist of Important Items and Information

Checklist of Important Items and Information

_____ First-aid kit

_____ Keys

_____ Parking permit

_____ Bell schedule

_____ School calendar of events

_____ Faculty meeting information

_____ Mailboxes

_____ Department meeting information

_____ Telephone

_____ Extracurricular information

_____ Supplies

_____ Teachers' association information

_____ Textbooks

_____ Personnel data for the school

_____ Mentor teacher/peer coach

_____ Duplicate department procedures

_____ Curriculum guides

_____ Substitute teacher folder

FORM 1.2. Classroom Design

Imagine Your Classroom on the First Day

❖ Student desks

❖ Class materials

❖ Lighting

❖ File cabinet

❖ Boxes

❖ Desk

❖ Tables

❖ Adult chairs

❖ Storage space

❖ _____

❖ _____

❖ _____

❖ _____

❖ _____

❖ Audiovisual equipment

❖ Music (CD player, cassette recorder, radio, etc.)

❖ Textbooks

❖ Telephones

❖ Mailboxes

❖ Technology

❖ Computers

❖ _____

❖ _____

❖ _____

❖ _____

❖ _____

FORM 1.3. Sample School Policies and Procedures Checklist

School Policies and Procedures Checklist

- ☐ Child abuse
- ☐ Injury report
- ☐ Medications
- ☐ Attendance
- ☐ Class coverage
- ☐ Field trips
- ☐ Report cards
- ☐ Progress reports
- ☐ Fire drill
- ☐ Earthquake/hurricane/tornado
- ☐ Other disaster procedures
- ☐ Student telephone use
- ☐ Assembly programs
- ☐ After-school hours
- ☐ Faculty meetings
- ☐ Professional development
- ☐ Extracurricular clubs and activities
- ☐ Academic calendar
- ☐ _____
- ☐ _____

Important People to Know

By now you have been able to wander the building, visualize your classroom, gather materials, meet personnel, and locate important supplies as you prepare for the first days of school.

There are many important people in a secondary classroom who will provide assistance to you. These people will have an influence in your classroom as well as on the content, classroom management, and delivery of instruction.

Important Telephone Numbers

Sometimes new teachers feel like they are stuck in the middle of a large bureaucracy in their district and school. The moment may arrive in which you need or require something in your classroom but you cannot find the necessary telephone numbers. To avoid this, complete Form 1.4 and keep it handy.

It is just when you need one location to bring the necessary resources together that you wish for a central telephone number for information. How do you contact payroll when your first check is late? Have your credentials and/or licenses been received by personnel? When are your tuberculin test results due to the district office? Whom do you call? How many days do you have available for sick leave? Who is assigned to new teachers? How do you contact that person? Complete Form 1.5 and keep it handy in case you ever need answers to questions such as these.

Some Questions Prior to the First Week of School

Building

- ◆ What time is the building opened? Closed?

- ◆ When do you receive a school map?

- ◆ How can you get in on weekends?

- ◆ Where are faculty meetings held? When is the first one?

FORM 1.4. Important Names and Phone Numbers

The principal

_____   _____
Name   Telephone Number

School secretary

_____   _____
Name   Telephone Number

Vice principal

_____   _____
Name   Telephone Number

Vice principal's secretary

_____   _____
Name   Telephone Number

Vice principal

_____   _____
Name   Telephone Number

Vice principal's secretary

_____   _____
Name   Telephone Number

Counselor(s)

_____   _____
Name   Telephone Number

_____   _____
Name   Telephone Number

Dean

_____   _____
Name   Telephone Number

Dean's secretary

_____   _____
Name   Telephone Number

Librarian

_____   _____
Name   Telephone Number

Department chair

_____   _____
Name   Telephone Number

Mentor teacher

_____   _____
Name   Telephone Number

Special education/
   IEP chairperson

_____   _____
Name   Telephone Number

Resource specialist

_____   _____
Name   Telephone Number

Professional growth
   advisor

_____   _____
Name   Telephone Number

(continued)

FORM 1.4. Continued

Classified support staff

Head custodian

_____   _____
                    Name   Telephone Number

Custodian

_____   _____
                    Name   Telephone Number

Technology technician

_____   _____
                    Name   Telephone Number

Attendance clerk

_____   _____
                    Name   Telephone Number

Library technician

_____   _____
                    Name   Telephone Number

Textbook technician

_____   _____
                    Name   Telephone Number

Nurse

_____   _____
                    Name   Telephone Number

Paraprofessional assistants

_____   _____
                    Name   Telephone Number

_____   _____
                    Name   Telephone Number

_____   _____
                    Name   Telephone Number

Parent volunteer assistants

_____   _____
                    Name   Telephone Number

_____   _____
                    Name   Telephone Number

_____   _____
                    Name   Telephone Number

Important others

_____   _____
                    Name   Telephone Number

_____   _____
                    Name   Telephone Number

_____   _____
                    Name   Telephone Number

_____   _____
                    Name   Telephone Number

FORM 1.5. Most Commonly Used Telephone Numbers

	Phone	Fax	E-mail
District office	_____	_____	_____
Credential office	_____	_____	_____
Personnel/payroll department	_____	_____	_____
Employee assistance program	_____	_____	_____
Instructional media department	_____	_____	_____
Teachers' association office	_____	_____	_____
Health information	_____	_____	_____
Mentor teacher program	_____	_____	_____
Curriculum services	_____	_____	_____
New teacher program advisor	_____	_____	_____
Educational technology	_____	_____	_____
_____	_____	_____	_____
_____	_____	_____	_____
_____	_____	_____	_____
_____	_____	_____	_____

Personal Absences

- Whom do you call first?
- Who has the paperwork regarding absences at your school site?
- What are the school procedures?

School Supplies

- How do you obtain emergency supplies?
- How do you use the photocopier? To whom do you go if it breaks down?
- How do you order audiovisual materials (films, study prints, videotapes, CD-ROMs, etc.)?
- Where are the field trip forms?
- Are there funds for purchasing supplies for the classroom? How much? With whom do you discuss this?

Classroom Supplies

- Do you have enough supplies?
- Can you obtain supplies from your department?
- Are there special forms for the district, school, or department?

**The first bell will ring soon.
Are you ready for your students?**

Dress for Success

You prepared your résumé, had a successful interview, and have been appointed to your first teaching position. It is now time to dress for the job.

The dress for a school and district will vary, so you need to note the dress of your colleagues prior to the first day or week of classes. It may be that the dress code is informal, but how informal is it? In any case, be sure to pay attention to your feet. A teacher walks and stands for hours without sitting down. You need to wear comfortable shoes and clothing that provide comfort while bending, sitting, and standing for long periods of time. If you teach art-related courses, you may need to wear clothing that may be changed at the end of the day.

Caring for Yourself

One must learn by doing the thing; for though you think you know it, you have no certainty until you try.

—Sophocles

There are many things to remember during the first month of school. It may seem that long ago are the days at the university! Your concerns were most likely employment, family, school, community service, and associated university duties.

Teaching is another story. Initially, it may seem like there is too much to do in very little time. You will need to organize, reorganize, and then reorganize again your limited time. The thought of going to bed early during the first weeks of school may disappear as you wish for more hours of the day and night.

Plan to set aside time during your day for recreational types of activities as well as something to refresh your nervous system. Your body will thank you for taking care of your "temple." Exercise, meditate, or share a cup of tea with a friend. Whatever you do, set aside time for yourself. Plan to get as much sleep and rest as you can into your schedule. Teaching is filled with the unknown, and you will need sleep, rest, and exercise to accomplish the daily tasks associated with the school day.

❖ FIGURE 1.1. Instructional Associates

General Questions

♦ What is my role in evaluating the paraprofessional?

♦ Is there a paraprofessional association or union involved?

♦ How will my students address paraprofessionals?

♦ What are the specific classroom procedures?

♦ What will be the daily routines?

♦ Will the paraprofessional be involved with grading?

♦ What about disaster drills?

♦ What authority does the paraprofessional have with discipline?

♦ What will be done if I am absent?

♦ Is there an exception that the paraprofessional attend meetings?

Professional Ethics

♦ Does the paraprofessional read student records?

♦ What about confidentiality of student information?

♦ What happens if we disagree?

Paraprofessional Assistance

There are school and district expectations established regarding paraprofessional assistance. It is important that you establish consistent communication. Find the time to plan with paraprofessionals and be prepared for them even if they are absent from your classroom (see Figure 1.1).

Educational philosophy and teaching priorities are key elements in providing clarity and consistency for the students in your classroom.

Special Education Students

It is a good idea to review the faculty roster to learn the names and locations of the special education teachers who will be your colleagues. The counseling department staff will alert you to any special needs of students in your classes. If you seek out the special education teachers, you can learn about the students, concerns, and issues in addition to the assistance that they might be able to provide you in your work.

Special education teachers can provide you with insights for parent-teacher conferences, and they can also provide you with information regarding district special education policies and assist in the identification of potential special education students in your classes.

English Language Learners

It is important to provide quality education for a diverse student population, and students at various secondary grade levels may be in different stages of learning the English language. There are a variety of programs to assist content-specific teachers for use in their secondary classrooms.

An instructional system of strategies that assists English language learners learn content while acquiring English is Sheltered English Instruction. Some students may attend your school and be involved in strategies in their content classes while attending your classes. Take the opportunity to learn which students in your class are receiving sheltered instruction. It might be useful to seek out and speak with your colleagues who have sheltered classes as well as learn new strategies to ensure that your curriculum is relevant, comprehensible, and integrated into your specific content area.

School Records

Each student in your class has records that can be found in a designated location at the school. The records may be found in the main office, vice-principal's office, or the counseling department. Learn where the records are stored and the type of student records that are kept. It may be the policy of your school or district to divide student records into specific offices. An example might be that the attendance records are kept in the vice principal's office, and the cumulative records are kept in the counseling department. If you have special education students in your classes, where are their records? Who is the custodian of those records?

Value the Differences in Your Classroom

A secondary classroom will reflect a variety of differences in the student population. To foster a friendly rapport that is consistent, respectful, and models a love of learning, the teacher must value and respect the students. There will be differences in the academic preparation, cultures, languages, and goals of the students in your classes. The secondary teacher must embrace differences and not discourage the students or their families. Maintaining respect for all students in the secondary classroom is crucial to academic learning.

Mailboxes

A teacher's mailbox is the location not only for mail but also a place for faculty members to meet for a brief encounter. This is the place where the veteran teachers will have the opportunity to engage in brief conversations about the life of the school.

A teacher's mailbox is filled with different types of mail, important and unimportant. Take the opportunity to visit your mailbox several times a day. Parent and student messages, as well as scheduled and unscheduled meeting messages, will be placed in your mailbox. Try to form a habit of reading your mail and emptying your mailbox on a daily basis.

Emergency Procedures

Once you are employed with your district, you will receive a large amount of paperwork. The emergency procedures may be found in the district paperwork or perhaps in the local school-site material. You should thoroughly read the expectations, routines, and procedures for emergencies. The teacher is expected to learn what to do before, during, and after a disaster.

Parking Registration Policies

Soon the bell will ring and the students will begin to arrive at your classroom. There is a lot to learn about the students in your classroom. For example, some of your students will own their own automobiles and drive to school.

You probably have noticed that there are two different parking lots at your school: One for the teachers, staff, and administrators, and a second parking lot for those students who drive their automobiles to and from school.

Parking regulations will differ from district to district. Are there automobile registration forms for teachers (see Form 1.6)? Who maintains the automobile registration information? Do you receive a ticket if parked in the student lot? Are there specific numbered or lettered parking spaces? What time are the student parking lot gates locked? To whom do you speak about a parking ticket if you should receive one? Are there parking lot personnel that you should know about?

"To-Dos" Before School Begins

To help you prepare for your first days of school, complete Form 1.7.

FORM 1.6. Sample Parking Registration Form

Parking Registration

Teacher _____
Last name   First name   Middle initial

E-mail address _____

Telephone   _____   _____
Home   School

Vehicle   Vehicle identification
make/model _____   number _____

License number_____   Color _____

Year_____   Other _____

Campus Assignment: Full time   /   Part time   /   Temporary   *(circle one)*

For office use

Issue date_____   Expiration date _____

Area/assignment space_____   Other _____

FORM 1.7. Sample To-Do Checklist Before School Begins

Before School Begins. . .

☐ Meet with administrators

☐ Meet with secretary and clerical staff

☐ Meet with your assigned teacher mentor to share information

☐ Meet with key school resource staff

☐ Meet with classroom paraprofessional

☐ Acquire copies of important school materials
(e.g., student handbook, facility orientation handbooks,
school policies, maps, bell schedules, disaster drills)

☐ Acquire school supplies for classroom

☐ Design the physical arrangement of the classroom

☐ Assemble referrals, passes, lunch slips, and so forth

☐ Locate important rooms (e.g., faculty lounge), copy machines,
library, audiovisual equipment, and so forth

☐ Obtain copies of lunch or brunch procedures for students

☐ Obtain copies of extra-duty responsibilities
(school clubs and organizations)

☐ Familiarize yourself with the food services routines
at the school

☐ Obtain keys for the classroom, office, and so forth

☐ Obtain technology supplies

(continued)

FORM 1.7. Continued

☐ Attend new-teacher orientation sessions

☐ Organize your parent contacts, newsletters, conference information, and substitute teacher preparation materials

☐ Acquire books, supplementary books, and materials

☐ Acquire copies of curriculum guide, class lesson plans, and so forth

☐ Obtain samples of unit plans and teachers' manuals

☐ Obtain field trip information

☐ Other: _____

☐ Other: _____

The First Week of School

Planning for the first day and week of school may seem over-whelming. There is much to remember and there may be many people who seem to know more than you do. Remember that, right now, many of the ideas, activities, and procedures are new to you, but eventually the classroom routine will become just that—routine!

There are many details that must be covered before school starts, and it is best to take small steps. Plan for the large picture but take small snapshots along the way. The first day of school will present new faces and challenges. Plan to arrive early your first day, and be well prepared and organized so that your classroom is efficient and effective (see Figure 2.1 and Forms 2.1 and 2.2).

1. What time is lunch?

2. How do I recognize the appropriate signals with my students' personalities?

3. Where is the staff restroom?

4. Am I really ready?

❖ **FIGURE 2.1.** Preparing for the First Week of School

Are you ready for your students? Have you . . .

1. Developed a preliminary daily schedule?

2. Planned for class procedures?

3. Created a seating chart?

4. Established your routines mentally and rehearsed them before the students arrive?

5. Written timelines for the first day and placed them in your plan book?

6. Read the names of your students from the attendance roster so that you can pronounce them on the first day?

7. Created a signal that all of the students in the class will recognize as important?

8. Planned your get-acquainted activity and welcome to the students?

9. Assembled the necessary classroom supplies?

10. Prepared the classroom environment so that it is inviting to students?

11. Established your classroom management plan?

12. Know how you plan to start your class?

13. Developed activities for your students that begin when they arrive?

14. Assembled necessary classroom forms?

15. Acquired the audiovisual and technology equipment you will need for the first month?

16. Read everything that you have received from the school and/or district?

17. Met with the necessary school staff, teachers, and classified members?

18. Created your gradebook?

19. Figured out how to use your classroom telephone?

20. Coordinated the use of materials with department colleagues?

21. Made sure you understand the school and district discipline policies, procedures, and processes?

FORM 2.1. Sample Daily Schedule Form

Daily Schedule

MONDAY	TUESDAY	WEDNESDAY	THURSDAY	FRIDAY

FORM 2.2. Sample Checklist of Things to Do

Things to Do

☐ Complete all of the district paperwork.

☐ Meet with the department chair to obtain course outline, curriculum materials, and resources for subject area.

☐ Meet with the library clerk to order content standards and curriculum materials.

☐ Meet with the textbook clerk to collect additional books for the new students.

☐ Meet with the audiovisual technician to order films and additional resources.

☐ Meet with the technology technician to review policies for ordering resources.

☐ Meet with the school nurse for first-aid supplies.

☐ Meet with the custodian for cleaning supplies, soap, and paper towels.

☐ Meet with the counselors to discuss special-needs students.

☐ Meet with the school psychologist regarding testing and district policies.

☐ Meet with the dean/vice-principal/principal for last minute details.

☐ Meet with a school representative to discuss academic support for students who may need tutoring or special assistance on or off campus.

☐ Meet with resource staff at the school site to provide additional assistance for special programs.

☐ Meet with the paraprofessionals assigned to your classroom.

☐ Prepare substitute folder for the office.

☐ _____

☐ _____

☐ _____

Class Procedures

The first day of school is tomorrow, and new and exciting things will take place. There also will be a few things that will not go as planned, so be prepared! (See Figures 2.2 through 2.4, and Forms 2.3 through 2.11).

❖ FIGURE 2.2. Sample Class Schedule #1: 50-Minute Period

Period: _____

Date: _____

9:00	Welcome Introduction of the teacher Class signals
9:05	Get-acquainted activity
9:20	Class signal/practice
9:20	Classroom management rules and classroom practices review
9:25	Daily schedule review ▷ Teacher expectations ▷ Student responsibilities
9:30	Fire drill and disaster procedures review
9:35	An introduction to your course worksheet ▷ Take roll, add students, and complete administrative tasks ▷ Complete interest and hobbies worksheet
9:45	Practice class signals
9:50	Bell rings— ▷ Next period in 7 minutes

You may have 5 minutes to get ready for the next period, so go to the restroom, speak to students, or get a bit of water in case your throat is dry.

FORM 2.3. Sample First-Day Schedule

Your First-Day Schedule

☐ Smile.

☐ Be prepared and know who is in which period.

☐ Have ample classroom supplies.

☐ Prepare for new students, absent students, and transfers from other classes and other schools.

☐ Smile.

☐ Review the daily schedule.

    ☐ Lesson plans

    ☐ Chalkboard

    ☐ Overhead

    ☐ Student handouts

    ☐ Technology presentation

☐ Review disaster procedure.

☐ Review fire drill procedures.

☐ Smile.

☐ Have an activity (get acquainted) for the students and yourself (share a bit of yourself).

☐ Review your classroom management system.

☐ Smile.

☐ Review signals for when class begins and ends.

❖ FIGURE 2.3. Sample Class Schedule #2: 50-Minute Period

Period: _____

Date: _____

9:00	Welcome Take your seats Listen for the bell Introduction of the teacher Daily schedule review Turn in homework or required school forms
9:10	Cooperative learning group activities
9:30	Whole-class sharing and reporting
9:40	Homework assignments
9:50	Closing End of the period

> **Place this schedule on the chalkboard or overhead so that your students are aware of the daily expectations, objectives, and assignments.**

Go to the restroom, speak to your students, stick your head outside the door, and take a deep breath! Here comes your next group of students!

FORM 2.4. Get-Acquainted Activity 1: People I Admire

People I Admire

Directions:

1. Meet with the person sitting next to you and together complete the Most Admired Person List.

2. You have 3 minutes each to share the names of three people that you most admire in the world. They may be living or dead.

3. Explain why these three people are important to you.

Most Admired Person List

1. _____

2. _____

3. _____

Importance

1. _____

2. _____

3. _____

Return this sheet to your teacher at the end of this activity.

Student _____   Subject _____

Date _____   Teacher _____

Period _____

SOURCE: From Scannell, E., & Newstrom, J. (1983). *More Games Trainers Play* ("Who Am I?," p. 27). New York: McGraw-Hill. Adapted with permission.

FORM 2.5. Get-Acquainted Activity 2: Most Unusual Happenings

Most Unusual Happenings

Directions:

1. Meet with the person sitting next to you and together complete the Unusual Happenings List.

2. You have 3 minutes each to share something unusual that has happened to you.

3. Explain why these three things are important.

Unusual Happenings List

1. _____

2. _____

3. _____

Importance

1. _____

2. _____

3. _____

Return this sheet to your teacher at the end of this activity.

Student _____   Subject _____

Date _____   Teacher _____

Period _____

SOURCE: From Scannell, E., & Newstrom, J. (1983). *More Games Trainers Play* ("Who Am I?," p. 27). New York: McGraw-Hill. Adapted with permission.

FORM 2.6. Get-Acquainted Activity 3: Favorite Television Program

My Favorite Television Program

Directions:

1. Take out a piece of paper and list the name of your two (2) favorite television programs.

2. Meet with a small group of students (no more than three) in this class and introduce yourself to the group.

3. The group will try to identify you based on one of your favorite television programs. You cannot tell them the name of the program; they must guess.

4. Do not give any clues to the group other than day, night, afternoon, or evening programming. You may not share whether it is a comedy, musical, or drama. They will try to guess based on your likes and dislikes about television programming this semester.

5. The group may ask general questions about your favorite program. They may ask specific questions about your likes and dislikes about television programming. They may also ask questions about the channel, such as MTV, VH-1, and so on.

6. When everyone in the group has been identified based on their favorite television program, be prepared to share this information with the entire class.

SOURCE: From Scannell, E., & Newstrom, J. (1983). *More Games Trainers Play* ("What's Your Name?," p. 27). New York: McGraw-Hill. Adapted with permission.

FORM 2.7. My Expectations for This Class

My Expectations for This Class

Today:

_____

_____

_____

_____

This Semester:

_____

_____

_____

_____

Grade:

The grade I expect to receive is _____ because I plan to:

_____

_____

Student _____

Period _____

Subject _____

Date _____

FORM 2.8. Sample Interests and Hobbies Worksheet

Interests and Hobbies

Period _____   Subject _____

Date _____   Name _____

Address _____   Phone Number _____

1. Why are you in this course this semester? _____
_____

2. What magazines are your favorites? _____

3. What newspaper do you read on a regular basis?_____

4. What are your favorite parts of the newspaper? _____

5. List the titles of the last three books that you read and enjoyed.

    a. _____

    b. _____

    c. _____

6. What are you good at doing?_____

7. What are three of your hobbies?

    a. _____

    b. _____

    c. _____

8. Do you have a job?_____ What kind of work do you do? _____

9. What do you plan to do after you graduate from high school? _____

10. Do you plan to attend college? _____

11. If so, what might you major in? _____

FORM 2.8. Continued

12. Have you given some thought to the type of job you would like to be doing 10 years from now? _____ What type of job is it? _____

13. What is your favorite class in school? _____

14. Do you have a driver's license? _____

15. Who are your favorite recording stars?

    a. _____

    b. _____

    c. _____

16. What are your favorite movies?

    a. _____

    b. _____

    c. _____

17. What are your favorite television programs?

    a. _____

    b. _____

    c. _____

18. What are the names of your favorite CDs?

    a. _____

    b. _____

    c. _____

19. What was your favorite grade in elementary school? _____

20. What do you enjoy doing after school? _____

Note: Be sure that you obtain permission from your school administrator prior to using this worksheet in case there are specific policies regarding student questionnaires.

FORM 2.9. Sample My Favorite Cities Worksheet

My Favorite Cities

Name   _____

Period   _____

Subject _____

Date   _____

My favorite three cities in the world are:

1. _____

2. _____

3. _____

My favorite three cities in the United States are:

1. _____

2. _____

3. _____

Describe three of your favorite cities.

1. _____

2. _____

3. _____

Write a paragraph about your favorite cities and explain what makes them so special to you.

FORM 2.10. Sample My Favorite Animal Worksheet

My Favorite Animal

Name   _____

Period   _____

Subject _____

Date   _____

If you could pose (safely) at Disney Studios for a publicity picture with the animal of your choice, which animal would you choose?

Animal _____

Describe the characteristics of your animal.

1. _____

2. _____

3. _____

On a separate sheet of paper:

Write a paragraph about your favorite animal and its characteristics. Be specific about the importance of this animal.

How is your personality similar to your favorite animal?

What is your least favorite animal? Why?

FORM 2.11. Sample My Favorite Color Worksheet

My Favorite Color

Name _____

Period _____

Subject _____

Date _____

My favorite color is _____

Describe your favorite color in three words.

1. _____

2. _____

3. _____

Write a paragraph about your favorite color and explain why you like it.

First Day of School Celebration Award

Congratulations! You survived the first day of school and now it is time to celebrate! Why not treat yourself and do one or more of the following:

- Meditate and take care of yourself spiritually.
- Take a long shower.
- Take a long bath with music and candles.
- Go shopping for something personal for yourself.
- Call your mother and father to share the day.
- Meet with your mentor teacher and share the day.
- Go out to dinner with a friend or family member.
- Go to an athletic club for a workout.
- Take your dog for a long walk.
- Go to bed an hour earlier than the previous night.
- Visit with another first-year teacher and celebrate together your first day of school.

Planning for Classroom Instruction

The first days of school are hectic. Think about how you have prepared for your students. If you overplan and feel that there is too much to do, your overplanning may work for you. For example, if you arrive at the end of your lesson plan for the day and there are still 15 minutes left in the period, you can cover some of your overplanned material during that extra time.

You may have also set up the classroom and feel ready. It may be a good idea to invite a student to sit in your classroom and help you find locations that may be a distraction.

The first days of school will go much faster than you expect. Avoid disorganization and plan! Plan for the expected! Plan for the unexpected! Plan!

1. Have you planned for the new students who will arrive the first week of school?

2. Do you have ample classroom supplies?

3. Do you have enough classroom furniture for your students?

Classroom Instruction

It is important that you plan for instruction. The planning process should include backup plans in addition to plans for teaching students of differing abilities. Be flexible and ready for surprises that may take place prior to the beginning of school.

Planning for classroom instruction involves knowing what materials, textbooks, supplies, supplemental materials, and technology is available to you and your students. It is practical to have a master list or inventory of your equipment for a variety of reasons (see Form 3.1). For example, your substitutes, students, parent volunteers, and teaching colleagues will be assisting you in the classroom, so it would be helpful to them to have access to a master list or inventory of equipment. Be aware of the materials and their uses for students. Organization and knowledge are essential during the first year of teaching. Your classroom organization can save you time and energy and propel your students to your next level of planning. It will assist volunteers, provide a vision and direction to classroom observers, and assist you in your short- and long-range planning for the academic year.

Are there some materials that might be useful to you within your district? Why not begin a list of those items, including vendor information (see Form 3.2). This list will be helpful to you when ordering outside as well as inside your district.

If you plan to teach certain units during the academic year, create a Fairy Godmother list and begin to list the materials and supplies that will be helpful in the implementation of your lessons (see Form 3.3). What about multimedia materials that you think might be useful? Sometimes you can find publishers' catalogs with materials that you might like to use in your classroom in the future. Write it all down!

Planning for Instruction

Clerical Responsibilities

What types of clerical needs do you think you will need for your class? Student helpers may be available to you. What do they do? Also, parent volunteers and paraprofessionals need to know what is expected of them. Take a few minutes and plan for your students as well as for your volunteers and paraprofessionals (see Form 3.4).

FORM 3.1. Sample Classroom Inventory Form

Classroom Inventory Form

Teacher _____   Subject _____

Period _____   Date _____

Room number_____

	Quantity	How to Obtain	Contact Person
Furniture ■ _____ ■ _____ ■ _____			
Audiovisual equipment (VCR, monitor, slide projector, etc.) 1. _____ 2. _____			
Audiovisual instructional 1. _____ 2. _____			
Computers/technology 1. _____ 2. _____			
Software 1. _____ 2. _____			
Supplies: basic 1. _____ 2. _____			
Supplies: supplementary 1. _____ 2. _____			
Books: regular texts 1. _____ 2. _____			
Books: supplementary 1. _____ 2. _____			

Arnold, H. *Succeeding in the Secondary Classroom.* © 2001. Corwin Press, Inc.

FORM 3.2. Sample Order Form

Order Form

Teacher _____   Subject _____

Period _____   Date _____

Room number _____

Item	Vendor	Address	Phone	Price	Total	Date Sent

Arnold, H. *Succeeding in the Secondary Classroom.* © 2001. Corwin Press, Inc.

FORM 3.3. Sample Wish List

Wish List

Arnold, H. *Succeeding in the Secondary Classroom.* © 2001. Corwin Press, Inc.

FORM 3.4. Sample Clerical Responsibility Checklist

Clerical Responsibility Checklist

☐ Take attendance

☐ Gather papers for each class period

☐ Filing and conserving papers

☐ Computer-generated worksheets

☐ Duplication

☐ Telephone calls to resources

☐ Letter writing

☐ Mail

☐ Student work (e.g., portfolios)

☐ School errands

☐ Library visits

☐ Other:_____

☐ _____

☐ _____

☐ _____

Lesson Planning

The resources available to assist you in the area of lesson planning vary from the textbooks that you use to newspapers, professional organizations, the Internet, friends and colleagues, and those resources you used during your preservice.

Lesson planning is personal and reflects the interests, needs, experiences, background, and knowledge of the students and the teacher. A school district may provide new teachers with guides for lesson planning that reflect the district vision, goals, and objectives. Some schools still provide lesson plan books or planning guides for new teachers.

The subject-specific lesson plans that can be found on the Internet are useful and provide new teachers with information and plans that have been developed by teachers and other resource personnel of universities and school districts. In choosing to develop your own lesson plan around a particular lesson, a format that might be useful for new teachers is provided for your use (see Form 3.5).

The instructional program for your subject area is important, and your school or district may provide a specific plan for your use. However, a lesson plan book is personal and can be useful to you as a new teacher. The items in your lesson plan book must reflect your own thinking and planning for your lessons (see Forms 3.6 through 3.11).

FORM 3.5. Sample Daily Lesson Plan Chart

Daily Lesson Plan Chart

	Monday	Tuesday	Wednesday	Thursday	Friday
Period 1					
Period 2					
Period 3					
Period 4					
Period 5					
Period 6					

FORM 3.6. Sample Daily Lesson Plan Form

Daily Lesson Plan Form

Title: _____

Grade: _____

Subject: _____

Overview: _____

Objectives:

1. _____

2. _____

3. _____

Curriculum standards:

1. _____

2. _____

3. _____

Materials/resources:

1. _____

2. _____

3. _____

Internet/Web information:

1. _____

2. _____

3. _____

(continued)

FORM 3.6. Continued

Activities:

1. _____

2. _____

3. _____

Homework:

1. _____

2. _____

Assessment/evaluation:

1. _____

2. _____

3. _____

Extension activities:

1. _____

2. _____

3. _____

Interdisciplinary activities:

1. _____

2. _____

3. _____

FORM 3.7. Sample Weekly Lesson Plan Chart

Weekly Lesson Plan Chart

Subject: _____

Week of: _____

	Monday	Tuesday	Wednesday	Thursday	Friday
Period 1 Assignments: Activities: Materials:					
Period 2 Assignments: Activities: Materials:					
Period 3 Assignments: Activities: Materials:					
Period 4 Assignments: Activities: Materials:					
Period 5 Assignments: Activities: Materials:					
Period 6 Assignments: Activities: Materials:					

FORM 3.8. Sample Homework Form

Homework

Student
Name _____   Date _____

Subject _____   Period _____

Assignment	Material to Be Reviewed	Student Responsibility	Date Completed	Comments
	☐ Book ☐ Workbook ☐ Video ☐ Computer disk ☐ Worksheet ☐ Answer key ☐ Other ☐ Map or other graphic organizer			
Assignment	**Material to Be Reviewed**	**Student Responsibility**	**Date Completed**	**Comments**
	☐ Book ☐ Workbook ☐ Video ☐ Computer disk ☐ Worksheet ☐ Answer key ☐ Other ☐ Map or other graphic organizer			

Arnold, H. *Succeeding in the Secondary Classroom.* © 2001. Corwin Press, Inc.

FORM 3.9. Sample Summary of Course/Unit Activities Form

Summary of Course/Unit Activities

Subject[a]	Activities	Data Points				Completed

Arnold, H. *Succeeding in the Secondary Classroom.* © 2001. Corwin Press, Inc.
Note: a. Content-standard ESLR (expected student learning results).

FORM 3.10. Sample Course Syllabus Form

Course Syllabus

Date: _____

Semester: _____

Period: _____

Course title: _____

Course description: _____

_____

Course objectives: _____

_____

Course goals: _____

_____

Course instructional methods: _____

_____

Grading policy: _____

Grading scale: _____

Homework: _____

_____

Absences and late assignments: _____

Make-up assignments: _____

Progress reports: _____

Teacher contact (dates, times, locations): _____

_____

FORM 3.11. Sample Unit Planning Worksheet

Unit Planning

Title:

Goals and rationale:

Content:

Major concepts:

Instructional objectives:

Timelines:

Instructional strategies:

Evaluation/assessment:

Resources:

Unit Planning

Your lesson plan book is a guide to assist you in planning instruction for your classroom. It can be detailed, organized, personalized, and dynamic. Technology can be used so that lesson plans are computer generated on a daily, weekly, or monthly basis.

Staying flexible in planning is important to teaching. Following is a sample of a social studies unit for high school teachers ("The Persian Gulf War," published with the permission of Julie Block, University of the Pacific, July 1999). If you have made units in your teacher preparation courses, now is the time to modify the units and use them in your classroom.

**A unit plan can be helpful and useful
in your instructional planning.**

BOX 3.1. Sample Unit Plan

I. TITLE

THE PERSIAN GULF WAR

II. UNIT GOAL AND RATIONALE

To have the students understand the basic concepts of the Persian Gulf War and how it fits in a historical context. This part of the world has always been a hot spot for war in the Middle Eastern nations and also other nations. It is important for the students to know that these are not just isolated cases, but they spill over into other parts of the world and affect all of us.

III. MANDATED CONTENT

♦ Learn basic physical geography and map reading skills.

♦ Understand the increasing influence of other nations in the daily life of the American citizen.

♦ Understand the traditional and contemporary roles foreign nations play in the growth of American culture.

IV. MAJOR CONCEPTS

♦ The connection of this war to other wars, similarities and differences

♦ Map skills

♦ How a war halfway around the world affects people in the United States

V. INSTRUCTIONAL OBJECTIVES AND TIMELINE

1. The students will be able to identify where the Gulf War took place and be able to identify key countries and cities on a map with 80% accuracy (3 days).

2. The students will be able to place the actions of Saddam Hussein in a historical context based on at least one previously studied action of a leader of a country at war in an in-class essay with 80% accuracy (9 days to learn, 1 day to write the essay).

3. The students will perform the differences and similarities between the causes of this war and at least one previously studied war through a role play between the two nations (5 days).

4. The students will describe their feelings on U.S. involvement and leadership in the Gulf War in a 2 to 3 page opinion paper that should be supported with facts (2 days).

Total: 20 days

(continued)

BOX 3.1. Continued

VI. INSTRUCTIONAL STRATEGIES

A. This unit will begin with a comparison and contrast of Vietnam (the previous unit) and the Middle East and will close with an in-class essay in which the students will compare and contrast the actions of Saddam Hussein with the actions of a previously studied leader of a country at war. The unit will include mostly nontraditional learning strategies, meaning there will be minimal book work and lecture. The focus will be on hands-on learning in which the students will be using their creativity and outside resources to learn about the Gulf War and how it fits in with previously studied wars.

B. Lesson plans

1. The unit will begin with comparing and contrasting the geography of Vietnam with that of the Middle East, specifically that of Iraq, Kuwait, and Saudi Arabia (which are similar). We will move into map skills, and the students will be required to draw freehand a map of the Middle East as accurately as possible. They will also be put into groups and assigned one of four countries to research and present to the class. Students will be allowed to choose what information they feel the class must know about the country in order to understand this unit, with my approval and help if they would like it.

2. The second part of the unit is understanding how this war is related to other wars we have studied. This will be done through a guest speaker (a veteran of the war or someone with vast knowledge of it), the viewing of CNN news clips (and writing a short opinion paper on both), writing summaries and analyses of five newspaper articles, which I have provided or they have found and read, and conducting an interview with a parent or some other adult who can tell the student how he or she felt about the war (preferably someone old enough to remember this war and at least one other one so that they can compare the two).

3. Next the students will produce a 2- to 3-page opinion paper on their feelings of U.S. involvement and leadership in the war. By now they should have some opinion because they have seen and heard a lot of different things from people involved. I will give them one day in the library to research exactly what role the United States played so that they have their facts straight, although they will have had some exposure to this already.

4. The fourth part of this unit is a 15- to 20-minute role play illustrating the similarities and differences between the Gulf War and one previously studied war. The students can be creative in their presentation of the material as long as it is accurate and they do it live (they are not allowed to videotape it at home and bring it in). They will be limited as to what props they may use because of space limitations, but this will only

BOX 3.1. Continued

force their creativity further. Students will have 2 days in class to prepare, and if they need more time, it will have to be done outside of class. We will take 3 days to perform the role plays to allow for ample time to change the props for each group and for them to perform.

5. The unit will end with an in-class essay comparing the actions of Saddam Hussein with the actions of another leader of a country at war that we have studied. The purpose of this is for the students to understand that leaders of nations at war either think about it the same way or they are completely opposite; they either want to or they don't. There is no middle ground, and each leader believes strongly in what he is doing. This must be illustrated in their essay, along with an analysis and comparison of the two wars the leaders were involved in. I will give students the question beforehand so that they can be thinking of ideas before they actually have to write it. I will even encourage them to write something ahead of time but will stress that this may not be brought into the classroom!

VII. EVALUATION PROCEDURES

This unit will be evaluated on a points system with the points given out for each individual assignment according to a rubric. There will be 500 points possible for this unit, broken down as follows:

Freehand maps	1 @ 25 pts. = 25
Country presentations	1 @ 25 pts. = 25
Newspaper article summaries	5 @ 5 pts. = 25
Opinion paper on guest speaker and CNN tapes	1 @ 25 pts. = 25
Interview	1 @ 50 pts. = 50
Opinion paper on U.S. involvement	1 @ 50 pts. = 50
Performance	1 @ 100 pts. = 100
In-class essay	1 @ 100 pts. = 100
Participation and effort	1 @ 100 pts. = 100

VIII. LEARNING RESOURCES

To effectively teach this unit, the students must have access to the following materials:

a. Pen, pencil, regular lined paper, and butcher paper

b. Newspapers

c. Video

d. A creative and innovative mind

(continued)

BOX 3.1. Continued

Daily Lesson Plans
(under the assumption of a 50-minute class period)

Day 1, Monday:

1. Bell work and administrative duties—2 minutes

2. Introduction to the unit; start with a discussion comparing and contrasting the geography of Vietnam, which we've already studied, and what the students think the geography of the Middle East is like; have whole class brainstorm on how they think the war strategies will be different using their prior knowledge from this class—15 minutes

3. Look at maps of the Middle East to become familiar with where the major countries involved in the conflict are (Iraq, Kuwait, and Saudi Arabia)—5 minutes

4. Put students into 6 groups of 5 that I choose; explain that each group will be responsible for 1 of 4 countries: Iraq, Kuwait, Saudi Arabia, or the U.S.; students must find out vital stats on these countries that would be pertinent to learning the relationship between them during the war; they will present these to the class on Wednesday; they are allowed, as a group, to determine what the other students need to know with my approval (and help if needed); class time will be allowed to work on it, but I will explain that they must work on the rest of it outside of class—20 minutes

5. Get students back to order and put the desks back where they should be; ask for any questions or clarifications; give a quick overview of the rest of the unit—8 minutes

6. Dismiss

Day 2, Tuesday:

1. Bell work and administrative duties—2 minutes

2. Hand out a couple of pieces of scratch paper to each student and explain that they will be drawing their own maps of the Middle East and can practice on this paper. I will hand out a copy of the map to each student; they must label all the countries and signify in some way the countries involved in the conflict (Iraq, Kuwait, and Saudi Arabia) along with the major cities (Baghdad, Kuwait City, and Riyadh); when they are ready to "do it for real," I will give them nice, white paper to draw their final product on—5 minutes

3. Give students the rest of the period to work on it and explain that they will have time to work on them tomorrow after the presentations; due on Friday; they also have the option of working on their presentations for the last 20 minutes of class—43 minutes

4. Dismiss

BOX 3.1. Continued

Day 3, Wednesday:

1. Start getting ready for presentations and administrative duties—5 minutes

2. Give presentations as groups while the rest of the class takes notes; about 5 minutes each—35 minutes (allow for lag time between groups)

3. Can work on their maps the rest of the period—10 minutes

4. Dismiss

Day 4, Thursday:

1. Bell work and administrative duties—2 minutes

2. Participatory review of previously studied wars—20 minutes

3. Discuss possible similarities and differences between this war and previously studied wars and why they are different or similar—10 minutes

4. One way it's different is that it was basically on TV; show CNN footage—15 minutes

5. Ask if the video changes their views at all and think about the influence of the media on the American citizens at home watching this; short discussion—3 minutes

6. Dismiss

Day 5, Friday:

1. Administrative duties; collect maps—2 minutes

2. Introduce guest speaker and explain they need to write a short opinion paper on the CNN video and the guest speaker (all in one paper), due on Monday—2 minutes

3. Guest speaker; question-and-answer period—46 minutes

4. Dismiss

Student Recordkeeping

There will be many opportunities for you to communicate with your students. Take the time to share with them your expectations, goals, and objectives on a regular and ongoing basis.

Student recordkeeping is a time-consuming requirement. Use technology to assist you or develop your own form. An important recordkeeping responsibility for a teacher is attendance accounting (see Form 4.1).

One of your goals should be to know who is in the class each period. You may receive your attendance period by period, but what about those new students in special education? The forms that are included in this chapter can provide you with some assistance during the first weeks of school.

You will receive an attendance sheet from the school.
You may modify it to reflect individual classes.

FORM 4.1. Sample Attendance Form

Attendance Form

Student	Program	Period	M T W T F	M T W T F	Comments— Special Programs	Total
					LEP RSP SDS Site Programs AVID ACAD	

Communicating With Students

The first week of school is the time to share with your students the different methods you will use to communicate with them.

Personal Appointments

Develop a schedule that will enable you to meet individually with your students. This can take place before or after school (see Form 4.2). You may also call students to have them share their interests, hobbies, and concerns about the class.

Small-Group Activities

A series of in-class, small-group activities during the first week of school can be valuable for the teacher and the students. They can begin to build feelings of trust and competition between the students and enable you to learn more about them.

Assignments and Routines

During the first of week of school, students should be informed of your expectations, routines, and procedures. Routines such as entering the classroom, using the restroom, sharpening pencils, using the classroom library, going to lockers, and other housekeeping routines should be communicated to students. Be sure that you teach them the rules and routines so that it is all understood.

Classroom Records and Telephone Log

Quickly learning your students' names is important, but you might have 150 students in your classroom per day! There are several ways to maintain your own records for students, such as file folders, teacher-made forms, and computer-generated programs that may assist you in remembering.

The students in your classes will bring different sets of skills, abilities, and expectations to your classroom. Make a decision to review their records prior to arrival or after you have had them in the classroom a short while.

Creating a recordkeeping system that works is important. Your department chair or department colleagues may recommend a system that is used by the school. In any case, a system that is developed by

FORM 4.2. Sample Personal Student Appointment Letter

Date: _____

Dear_____ :

You have an appointment before school at 7:45 a.m. on _____ in room _____ with your teacher. This appointment is for 10 minutes, and during that time we will discuss your involvement in _____ course and the Interest Form that you completed in class.

Sincerely,

_____
[Teacher's name]

you may work best. For example, create a telephone log to assist you when planning for conferences with students and parents (see Form 4.3). It is a method that is easy to use, and it is a quick reference for the teacher.

Student Contact

Create a method for making student contact on a regular or individual basis. This can mean creating different classroom activities for large groups, small groups, or individuals.

Developing a system of student contact and in-class response is important to your growth as a teacher (see Forms 4.4 and 4.5). It will provide you with positive ongoing relationships and communications with your students. Adolescents may often feel that they are just one of several students in your class, but ongoing student contact can break the initial barriers and maintain positive relationships.

Student Assessment of the Course and Homework

An informal method of receiving feedback from the students will be helpful as you plan your daily instruction (see Forms 4.6 and 4.7).

It is also a good idea to require students to keep track of their own homework assignments and grades (see Forms 4.8 through 4.10). To help facilitate this, use passes as a reward system (see Form 4.11). The extra credit and amnesty passes can be issued to students in a graduated fashion.

FORM 4.3. Sample Parent-Student Telephone Log

Parent–Student Telephone Log

Student/Parent	Telephone Number	Date	Time	Reason

FORM 4.4. Sample Student Contact Letter

Date: _____

Dear: _____

Welcome to my class!

This is my first year at _____ School and I am looking forward to providing you with an interesting and challenging class. You should plan to be on time and be prepared to participate in all class activities.

We will be covering the following this semester:

a. _____

b. _____

c. _____

d. _____

During the course of the first month of school, we will be discussing your grades and expectations. If you have any questions, please discuss them with me during my preparation period or after school from 3:00 p.m. to 4:00 p.m. daily.

Again, welcome to Room _____!

Sincerely,

_____
      [Teacher's name]

Arnold, H. *Succeeding in the Secondary Classroom.* © 2001. Corwin Press, Inc.

FORM 4.5. Sample Student Contact Log

Student Contact Log

Student	Period	Date	Comments

Arnold, H. *Succeeding in the Secondary Classroom.* © 2001. Corwin Press, Inc.

FORM 4.6. Sample Classroom Assessment Form

Classroom Assessment Form

Making _____ Better
[insert subject]

I liked _____ this week/month.

I disliked _____

I would change _____

by_____

_____

_____

How is your teacher doing?

5	4	3	2	I
Excellent	Very good	Alright	Could be better	Needs change

FORM 4.7. Sample Lesson Adjustment Form

Lesson Adjustment Form

Student: _____

Subject: _____

Date: _____

	What I liked about this lesson:	**What I would change about this lesson:**
1.		
2.		
3.		
4.		
5.		

FORM 4.8. Generic Weekly Homework Form

Weekly Homework Form

Student: _____

Subject: _____

Dates: _____

Week of: _____

Monday	Assignment?
	Due date?
Tuesday	Assignment?
	Due date?
Wednesday	Assignment?
	Due date?
Thursday	Assignment?
	Due date?
Friday	Assignment?
	Due date?

FORM 4.9. Assorted Classroom Passes

Homework Pass This pass entitles _____ to have lunch with the teacher for completing your homework on time.	**Homework Pass** This pass entitles _____ to have lunch with the teacher for completing your homework on time.
Extra Credit Pass This pass entitles _____ to go to the library for the entire period for completing additional assignments for this class.	**Extra Credit Pass** This pass entitles _____ to go to the library for the entire period for completing additional assignments for this class.
Amnesty This pass entitles _____ to come in on _____ to retake an examination/quiz for _____.	**Amnesty** This pass entitles _____ to come in on _____ to retake an examination/quiz for _____.

FORM 4.10. Sample Daily Student Grade Form

Daily Student Grade Form

Student: _____

Subject: _____

Date: _____

	Monday	Tuesday	Wednesday	Thursday	Friday	Total Points	Letter Grade
Week 1							
Week 2							
Week 3							
Week 4							
Week 5							

White: Teacher
Canary: Classroom file
Goldenrod: Student

Directions:
Press hard so that your copy is included in your classroom file for parent conferences.

NOTE: This form should be prepared in triplicate.

FORM 4.11. Sample Student Reading Record

Student Reading Record

	Title of Book/Article/Reading Chapter	Date Started	Date Finished	Student Evaluation
1.				☺ ☹
2.				☺ ☹
3.				☺ ☹
4.				☺ ☹
5.				☺ ☹
6.				☺ ☹
7.				☺ ☹
8.				☺ ☹
9.				☺ ☹
10.				☺ ☹
11.				☺ ☹
12.				☺ ☹

Classroom Management and Discipline

Classroom Environment

Several books have been written about the importance of bulletin boards in the classroom. Remember that a portion of the classroom, especially the bulletin board, should be shared with the students in your classroom.

Take the time to discuss the sharing of the bulletin board with your students. It would be interesting to develop a semester theme or period for the subject area. Also, students tend to take note of their own and their friends' work when it is displayed on a bulletin board so consider displaying their work.

Creativity of both the teacher and the students reflects organization, planning, and sensitivity to the cultures of the students; it does not mean a collection of travel posters from an airline. The construction of bulletin boards requires that time be set aside to plan, organize, and construct a bulletin board that is conducive to a positive student learning environment (see Form 5.1).

Is your classroom a reflection of your students?

FORM 5.1. Sample Bulletin Board Checklist

Bulletin Board Checklist

☐ Student display

☐ Daily schedule (rally schedules, minimum days)

☐ Attendance policies

☐ Classroom expectations and rules

☐ Disaster and fire drills

☐ Emergency information

☐ Unit plan themes

☐ Student announcements

☐ Special school holidays

☐ Seasonal themes (fall, winter, spring, summer)

☐ Special student holidays (e.g., birthdays, sports events)

☐ Student of the Month/Week

☐ Students of the Month/Week

☐ Interdisciplinary curriculum activities

☐ Other:_____

☐   _____

☐   _____

✧ FIGURE 5.1. Classroom Expectations

Set up your classroom expectations so that they are:

♦ Fair

♦ Clear

♦ Respectful

♦ Reflect high expectations

♦ Simple

♦ Consistent

Classroom Management

It is now time to think about how to organize and manage the students in your classroom. To create an orderly classroom, you must give much time to planning for the entire academic year, and you must give much thought to the atmosphere and climate of the classroom. There will be five or more different periods during the course of a day. The teacher must be fair, demonstrate a positive attitude, clearly communicate, and respect the students (see Figures 5.1 and 5.2). Consistency is important in the secondary classroom, so your success as a first-year teacher depends also on your classroom management plans. Students will recognize and respond to inconsistency, so it is your responsibility to make sure that the atmosphere of the classroom is one of respect, fairness, and consistency for each student (see Forms 5.2 through 5.3).

Where do you want to focus your classroom?

1. Do you want the students to come on a daily basis?

2. Do you want students to be on time?

3. Is it the student's responsibility to complete assignments on a regular and timely basis?

4. Do you want students on task?

5. Do you want the students quiet?

(text continues on page 79)

❖ FIGURE 5.2. Student and Teacher Bad Day Diagram

Is It Me?

Is it the Behavior of the Student?

Think

What Should I Do? What Behaviors Do We Want To Change?

Talk About It With The Class

Next Steps?

What Is My Reaction?

How Are The Students Reacting? Where Do We Start?

What Behaviors Do We Change?

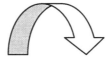

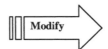

Review   Modify    Change

FORM 5.2. Sample Classroom Ownership Form

Classroom Ownership

This classroom belongs to Miss Smith and

1.
2.
3.
4.
5.
6.
7.
8.
9.
10.
11.
12.
13.
14.
15.
16.
17.
18.
19.
20.
21.
22.
23.
24.
25.
26.

This bulletin board begins with the teacher on the first day of class. After all students agree to the class rules, individual names will be added to share in the pride, accomplishments, and ownership of this classroom.

FORM 5.3. Sample Classroom Management Planning Form

Classroom Management Planning Form

Rules:

1.

2.

3.

4.

5.

Procedures:

1.

2.

3.

4.

5.

Consequences:

1.

2.

3.

4.

5.

Reflection:

Arnold, H. *Succeeding in the Secondary Classroom.* © 2001. Corwin Press, Inc.

6. When do you want the students to take their assigned seats? At the bell? Use of a teacher signal?

7. Do you want the students to respect each other?

8. Do you want to allow talking?

9. Do you want the students to keep their hands, feet, tongue, and objects to themselves?

10. What happens when students put down others? Are there consequences? If so, what are they?

11. Do you want students to raise their hands when they have questions?

12. How are consequences for negative behaviors discussed and maintained in your classroom? What are the negative behaviors in your classroom? Who designs or assists in naming the negative behaviors (the teacher or the teacher and students as a team)? Are there point deductions assigned to the consequences? Loss of privileges? Additional assignments? Telephone calls to parents?

If you attend a professional seminar or meeting and you hear about an idea that might be useful, list it on the Classroom Management Ideas Form (see Form 5.4). You might try it later in the year.

Classroom Tardy Policy

Following is a sample of a classroom tardy policy.[1]

First-time tardy: Student is allowed two tardies for the entire semester grading period/quarter.

Second-time tardy: After the two allowed tardies are used, the next time the student arrives to class late, he or she must stay in the classroom with the teacher for lunch for a minimum of 30 minutes. Also, the student's name is placed on the chalkboard so that all of the students are aware that the teacher will have a luncheon date.

Third- and fourth-time tardy: The student will again remain in the classroom at lunch for detention with the teacher.

Fifth-time tardy: After the fifth tardy, the student will be referred to the administration for Saturday school. Specifics regarding the period of time and required activities for Saturday school are in keeping with school and district policies. If there is no Saturday

FORM 5.4. Sample Classroom Management Ideas Form

Classroom Management Ideas

Colleagues in my department:

1.

2.

3.

4.

5.

Colleagues at my school:

1.

2.

3.

4.

5.

My mentor teacher:

1.

2.

3.

4.

5.

Others:

1.

2.

3.

4.

5.

school in the school/district, the next administrative step taken will be that of the policy of the school/district.

A student may also have a participation portion of the grade or points deducted from his or her grade for every tardy. This can be useful for those habitual students in your classroom.

Quote of the Day

Some teachers bring in a quote on the first day of class and share it with the students. This quote can be a foundation for the rules of the class and the expected behavior of all of the students. It is a demonstration of respect and of building a positive attitude among the students. If you choose to share quotes with your students, take the following steps:

1. During the first week of school, have a quote on the chalkboard or overhead projector prior to the arrival of the students.

2. The quote should be positive and uplifting to you as well as to the students.

3. Ask the students to take 5 to 7 minutes to discuss the significance of the quote, answering the question, "How does this quote relate to our class?"

4. Ask the students to share their discussions with the entire class.

5. Invite the students to bring in a quote that can be posted.

6. Build a library of the positive quotes for the classroom.

Note

1. Tardy policy adapted from the Hewlett Foundation-funded secondary beginning teacher grant. Reprinted with the permission of former beginning teacher Marianne Lawrence.

Working With Colleagues, Substitutes, and Paraprofessionals

When the bell rings on the first day of school, a new reality will begin for you. There will be opportunities to meet new friends who may become lifelong colleagues. There also will be opportunities to develop relationships with veteran teachers and colleagues at your school.

In addition to students, parents, and administrators, expect to work with paraprofessionals and substitute teachers. The instructional planning for a substitute will take a lot of your time, and planning for a substitute will be another new experience.

1. Reach out to colleagues for assistance.

2. Seek out mentors and opportunities to share with other first-year and veteran teachers.

Mentor Teacher

As you begin your first year of teaching, your district, school, or department may assign a mentor teacher to provide you support for the academic year. A mentor teacher can provide you with emotional and moral support as well as assist you in collision avoidance. Yes, there will be times when you want answers to simple questions such as what time is lunch, what is a rally-day bell schedule, or which celebrations are important at school.

Support by a Veteran Teacher

In addition to your mentor teacher, individual veteran teachers in your own department can offer you support . The teachers in your department know the ropes, and they can provide content-specific subject area assistance whether it be unit plans, textbooks, supplemental resources, or guest speakers to enhance your daily instructions.

A veteran teacher can be an asset in providing support regarding specific students. For example, perhaps you think a particular student is a problem only in your classroom. By working with veteran colleagues, you can learn if this student operates in the same manner in all of his or her other classes. You are probably not alone!

Substitute Teachers

The need for a substitute during the course of the academic school year should be planned for in advance (see Forms 6.1 and 6.2). You may become ill, your car may have a flat tire, or you may be involved in some type of professional development activity. Planning for a substitute is important if he or she is to maintain the routines and stability of your class in your absence.

When planning ahead for a substitute, your district or school may have specific forms and/or material for you to complete. A substitute teacher will try to provide instruction to your students based on the lesson plans that you prepare for such occasions.

1. Planning for a substitute takes time.

2. A substitute teacher is a person unknown to the students and yourself.

3. Take the time to provide the substitute with materials, paperwork, and pertinent information to help the class run smoothly in your absence.

FORM 6.1. Sample Substitute Teacher Checklist, I

Substitute Teacher Checklist

☐ Bell schedules

☐ Duty roster

☐ Current class lists

☐ Seating charts

☐ Emergency procedures

☐ Attendance procedures

☐ School-pass procedures

☐ List of reliable students (by class period)

☐ Audiovisual equipment procedures

☐ Map of the school

☐ Map of your classroom

☐ School forms

☐ Students who leave early

☐ Students who arrive late

☐ Students who need special attention

Location of:

☐ Staff lounge

☐ Restrooms

☐ Department workroom

☐ Cafeteria

Classroom management procedures:

☐ Signals

☐ Severe behavior

☐ Contacts in the school office

☐ Any necessary forms

FORM 6.2. Sample Substitute Teacher Checklist, II

Substitute Teacher Checklist

☐ Lesson planning:

    ☐ Daily plans

    ☐ Weekly plans

    ☐ Emergency plans

☐ Sets of fun activities

☐ Extra teaching ideas

☐ Teachers' manuals

☐ Paper and pencils

☐ Classroom supplies

☐ School personnel telephone information:

School secretary _____

Vice principal _____

Counselor _____

Department chair _____

Custodian _____

Principal _____

☐ Professional assistance from colleagues:

Teacher _____ Room number _____ Phone number _____

Teacher _____ Room number _____ Phone number _____

Teacher _____ Room number _____ Phone number _____

☐ Paraprofessional assistance:

Name _____ Room number _____ Phone number _____ Period___

☐ Parent/volunteer assistance:

Name _____ Period _____ Day(s) _____

Substitute Teacher Expectations

It is important that you return to an orderly, productive classroom after your absence. For this to happen, the expectations for the substitute must be clear. Create a substitute plan book, which can be a binder, folder, large envelope, or a file, and be sure that you are relaxed and have the time to prepare a plan that is easy to follow. Following are some questions to help you determine whether your substitute plan book is complete:

1. Did you ask the substitute to leave you a note explaining what happened in your absence?

2. If you want the substitute to correct student work and collect and leave the work in a specific location, did you write this in your plan?

3. Are there specific class procedures that you want followed?

4. Do you want the lesson plan followed? What happens if the students finish early?

5. What about enforcement of discipline policies?

6. How do you want the classroom to look at the end of the day?

7. Do you want student work organized by the period, subject, or both?

8. What about parents who contact the substitute? Where do you want that information?

9. What about your mail? Do you want it to remain in your mailbox?

10. What about your desk and personal items? Do you want the substitute to know which areas are off limits to students?

11. Which of your professional colleagues can the substitute contact in an emergency?

12. Do you want an inventory of class supplies to ensure that they are not lost?

Communicating With Colleagues

Your colleagues in your department can be very helpful to you during your teaching career. If you have questions, ask them! Meet regularly with your mentor teacher and any other veteran teacher who is assigned to you, and be sure to speak with other first-year teachers and share!

Communicating With Paraprofessionals: Instructional Associates

During the first week of school, you will meet the paraprofessional assigned to your classroom. If possible, try to obtain his or her name and telephone number and set up a meeting prior to the first week of school.

The purpose of the initial meeting is for the two of you to become acquainted with each other. It is important that paraprofessionals understand your philosophy, expectations, and procedures for the classroom, and on the other hand, you need to become aware of the district and union policies.

Schedule a series of meetings with the paraprofessional assigned to your classroom. Becoming a team and working together can be beneficial for your students, so sit down together and discuss areas such as discipline, professional ethics, confidentiality, and philosophy (see Figure 6.1 and Form 6.3).

✧ FIGURE 6.1. Areas for Discussion

1. School rules
2. Professional ethics
3. Philosophy
4. Supplies
5. Discipline
6. Teacher facilities on campus
7. Classroom management
8. Audiovisual and duplication equipment
9. Teaching knowledge
10. Child and adolescent development
11. Content and knowledge
12. Classroom policies
13. Parent contact
14. Student contact
15. Sharing of classroom information with others
16. Field trips
17. Personal items
18. Professional development
19. Emergency procedures
20. Child Abuse Reporting
21. Use of technology in the classroom
22. Class schedule (daily, weekly, monthly)
23. Reoccurring appointments (dental, medical)
24. Vacation schedule
25. Hobbies and interests

FORM 6.3. Sample Paraprofessional Student Assistance Inventory Form

Paraprofessional Student Assistance Inventory Form

Once the students arrive in your classroom,
what do you need assistance with?

☐ 1. Tutoring

☐ 2. Meeting

☐ 3. Small-group instruction

☐ 4. Homework catch up

☐ 5. Working with special-needs students

☐ 6. Working with second-language lessons

☐ 7. Computer technology

☐ 8. Reading assignments

☐ 9. Parent contacts

☐ 10. _____

☐ 11. _____

☐ 12. _____

☐ 13. _____

☐ 14. _____

Communicating
With Parents

The teaching journey is not a solo trip. There are numerous individuals who are a part of the journey. During a new teacher's first year, it may seem like there are too many people to get to know, but this is partially because everything is new. The students and their parents or guardians are important contacts the first year and each year thereafter. You should develop a positive working relationship with the parents of your students.

Parents and guardians must know that you value and respect their children. Let parents know that you wish to work with them in a mutually respectful fashion. Also let them know how you will provide learning experiences that will enhance the cognitive growth and development of their children.

Parent Contact

Parents are keenly interested in the progress of their children. The early years of preschool and elementary school involved active parent-teacher contact. Sometimes secondary teachers are unaware that students may distort the classroom picture. Parents seek information about the secondary classroom that is clear and accurate, and sending a parent letter is a method of introducing yourself and providing information (see Forms 7.1 and 7.2).

Planning for Open House

A monthly newsletter or flyer is useful in communicating to parents on a regular basis. This is an activity that can be used to introduce units of study, special days, classroom events, and requests for special supplies (see Figure 7.1). Include articles from the students so that they can take a part in creating the newsletter (see Figures 7.2 and 7.3). Regular notices sent to parents can also prepare parents and students for open house.

The period set aside for open house can provide an opportunity to share information, involve parents in the classroom activities, and assist the parents in understanding the importance of your subject area.

Communicating With Mom and Dad

The parents of your students are your partners, and the district and school expect you to establish and maintain ongoing communication with these parents. During the first weeks of school, you might contact the parents and provide them with information about your class (see Form 7.3).

An Introduction Letter

Prepare a letter of introduction to the parents, and inform them of your classroom procedures and policies (see Form 7.4). The letter should be sent early in the semester and might include homework, discipline, absence, and behavioral standards. In addition, specific curriculum projects, schedules, field trips, and special activities may be included in the letter as well as a mention of any professional development seminars that will take you away from the class.

FORM 7.1. Sample First Parent Contact Letter

Date: _____

Dear Parent:

My name is Ann Brown. I am your son/daughter's _____
                                                  [insert subject here]
teacher this year. I am pleased to join the faculty and look forward to meeting with you in the near future.

If you wish to contact me at school, please call me at 111-4444 during 3rd period (11:00 - 11:45 a.m.). This is my preparation period. I am also available after school from 3:00 to 4:00 p.m. daily.

It is a pleasure to become a member of _____ Middle/High School
                                          [school name]
and have the opportunity to teach your son/daughter.

Sincerely,

_____
[Teacher's name]

FORM 7.2. Sample Parent-Teacher Conference Log

Parent-Teacher Conference Log

Student	Subject	Period	Date	Time	Reason

❖ FIGURE 7.1. Parent Contact Newsletter: Sample Layout

SOCIAL STUDIES NEWSLETTER   October 1999

A monthly newsletter prepared by the students at Brown High School, Room 321.

Open House

on

Wednesday October 2, 1999

7:00 p.m.– 8:30 p.m.

Plan to attend!

Letter from Our Teacher

Notes from the Classroom

Lunch Menu for October

❖ FIGURE 7.2. Sample Newsletter

Social Studies
Room 5

Newsletter Title

January 2001

Lead Story Headline

This story can fit 175-225 words.

The purpose of a newsletter is to provide specialized information to a targeted audience. Newsletters can be a great way to market your product or service, and also create credibility and build your organization's identity among peers, members, employees, or vendors.

First, determine the audience of the newsletter. This could be anyone who might benefit from the information it contains, for example, employees or people interested in purchasing a product or requesting your service.

You can compile a mailing list from business reply cards, customer information sheets, business cards collected at trade shows, or membership lists. You might consider purchasing a mailing list from a company.

If you explore the Publisher catalog, you will find many publications that match the style of your newsletter.

Next, establish how much time and money you can spend on your newsletter. These factors will help determine how frequently you publish the newsletter and its length. It's recommended that you publish your newsletter at least quarterly so that it's considered a con-

sistent source of information. Your customers or employees will look forward to its arrival.

Caption describing picture or graphic.

Special points of interest:

✓ Briefly highlight your point of interest here.

✓ Briefly highlight your point of interest here.

✓ Briefly highlight your point of interest here.

✓ Briefly highlight your point of interest here.

Inside this issue:

Inside Story	2
Inside Story	2
Inside Story	2
Inside Story	3
Inside Story	4
Inside Story	5
Inside Story	6

Secondary Story Headline

This story can fit 75-125 words.

Your headline is an important part of the newsletter and should be considered carefully.

In a few words, it should accurately represent the

contents of the story and draw readers into the story. Develop the headline before you write the story. This way, the headline will help you keep the story focused.

Examples of possible headlines include Prod-

uct Wins Industry Award, New Product Can Save You Time!, Membership Drive Exceeds Goals, and New Office Opens Near You.

❖ FIGURE 7.3. Sample Newsletter

Inside Story Headline

This story can fit 150-200 words.

One benefit of using your newsletter as a promotional tool is that you can reuse content from other marketing materials, such as press releases, market studies, and reports.

While your main goal of distributing a newsletter might be to sell your product or service, the key to a successful newsletter is making it useful to your readers.

A great way to add useful content to your newsletter is to develop and write your own articles, or include a calendar of upcoming events or a special offer that pro-

motes a new product.

You can also research articles or find "filler" articles by accessing the World Wide Web. You can write about a variety of topics but try to keep your articles short.

Much of the content you put in your newsletter can also be used for your Web site. Microsoft Publisher offers a simple way to convert your newsletter to a Web publication. So, when you're finished writing your newsletter, convert it to a Web site and post it.

Caption describing picture or graphic.

Inside Story Headline

This story can fit 100-150 words.

The subject matter that appears in newsletters is virtually endless. You can include stories that focus on current technologies or innovations in your field.

You may also want to note business or economic trends, or make predictions for your customers or clients.

If the newsletter is distributed internally, you might comment upon

new procedures or improvements to the business. Sales figures or earnings will show how your business is growing.

Some newsletters include a column that is updated every issue, for instance, an advice column, a book review, a letter from the president, or an editorial. You can also profile new employees or top customers or vendors.

"To catch the reader's attention, place an interesting sentence or quote from the story here."

Inside Story Headline

This story can fit 75-125 words.

Selecting pictures or graphics is an important part of adding content to your newsletter.

Think about your article and ask yourself if the picture supports or enhances the message you're trying to convey. Avoid selecting images that appear to be out of context.

Microsoft Publisher includes thousands of clip art images from which you can choose and import into your newsletter. There are also several tools you can use to draw shapes and symbols.

Caption describing picture or graphic.

Once you have chosen an image, place it close to the article. Be sure to place the caption of the image near the image.

FORM 7.3. Sample Parent Communication Checklist

Parent Communication Checklist

☐ 1. Do I have a copy of the parent handbook?

☐ 2. How will I communicate with the parents of my students?

☐ 3. Are there district policies about parent communication?

☐ 4. Are there school policies about parent communication?

☐ 5. How will I document parent communication?

☐ 6. Will I keep a parent communication journal?

☐ 7. Will I keep a telephone parent communication log?

☐ 8. Will I develop a classroom newsletter?

☐ 9. When is open house? What do I do?

☐ 10. When are parent-teacher conferences?

☐ 11. Do I involve students in parent conferences?

☐ 12. Where are the forms located in the school for parent conferencing?

☐ 13. What are the procedures for homework and parent communication?

☐ 14. Other: _____

☐ 15. _____

☐ 16. _____

FORM 7.4. Sample Introductory Letter to Parents

Date: _____

Dear Parents:

It is a pleasure to teach at _____ High School this year. I teach _____
during _____ period this semester.
      (period number)
                                                     (course)

Attached to this letter is a copy of my syllabus so that you might be aware of the course expectations. Please be aware that homework is required on a weekly basis, so you might want look for these assignments. The daily schedule for the class is posted on the chalkboard on a daily basis. This provides each student with an opportunity to review the in-class assignments and the homework assignments before the end of the class period.

Please feel free to contact me during my preparatory periods, which are the 4th and 5th periods this semester. I am also free after school for telephone conferences every day except Wednesdays and Fridays. These are professional development days that include our weekly faculty meeting.

There will be several special activities this semester and a parent survey will be sent to you in the near future. In addition, I look forward to meeting you during the fall open house.

This will be a great year and I look forward to your assistance and support.

Sincerely,

_____
      [Teacher's name]

_____ Extension _____
(phone number)

Parent Conferences

A letter or other form of written communication sent to parents can be helpful in preparing for parent conferences. Parents can respond to classroom and curriculum issues to prepare for these conferences. The conferences may be district conferences, school parent-teacher conferences, or they may be conferences set up on an as-needed basis.

Parent Volunteer Survey

A survey sent to parents can communicate your needs for volunteers and how they can be useful in the classroom (see Form 7.5). Include at-home projects in the survey as well as encouraging class volunteer activities for working parents.

Parent Involvement Programs

A positive parent attitude and support are important and conducive to enhancing student learning. Take responsibility in making efforts to inform parents so that they understand and develop a picture of their child's learning.

Telephone Calls

A positive telephone call home to parents about their child can establish a good relationship with parents. Keep a telephone log and do not call parents only about negative behavior but also call to report positive behavior and to ask for assistance for programs or projects for your class (see Form 7.6). Telephone calls to parents can be useful in problem solving and conflict resolution.

Positive Communication Forms

The development of shared responsibility concerning student success between parents and a teacher will pay dividends for student success. Use communication forms to create a two-way communication system that is regular and consistent, which can achieve positive results for the student, parents, and teacher (see Forms 7.7 and 7.8).

Personal thank-you notes to parents demonstrate that you appreciate their efforts in the classroom. This communication is warm and can be sent after a specific event, project, program, or improved progress of a student.

FORM 7.5. Sample Parent Volunteer Survey

Parent Volunteer Survey

Course: _____ Period: _____

Semester: _____ Teacher: _____

Parent name: _____

Home phone: _____ Work phone: _____

Fax number: _____ E-mail address: _____

Availability: _____

Day(s) _____ Time(s) _____ Evenings only _____

Interests

- ☐ 1. Field trip supervision
- ☐ 2. Curriculum projects
- ☐ 3. Assisting in the classroom
- ☐ 4. Special events and celebrations
- ☐ 5. At-home projects
- ☐ 6. Telephone tree about special programs and projects
- ☐ 7. Class photographer
- ☐ 8. Guest speaker
- ☐ 9. Driving students on special trips and projects
- ☐ 10. Art projects and related activities
- ☐ 11. Music projects and related activities
- ☐ 12. Library projects
- ☐ 13. Interdisciplinary programs and projects
- ☐ 14. Other: _____

Please complete and return no later than _____ by fax, U.S. mail, e-mail,
(date)
or with your child. Thank you for your time and support of our classroom.

FORM 7.6. Sample Parent Telephone Log

Parent Telephone Log

Date: _____

Time: _____

Telephone: _____

Student: _____

Subject: _____

Period: _____

Concerns:

1.

2.

3.

Solutions:

1.

2.

3.

Comments:

_____

_____

_____

FORM 7.7. Sample Positive Parent–Teacher Communication Form

Positive Parent–Teacher Communication Form

Student name: _____

Course: _____ Period: _____

Semester: _____ Date: _____

The good news is that _____

_____

_____

_____

_____

_____

_____

FORM 7.8. Sample Teacher Communication Form

Teacher Communication Form

Student name: _____

Course: _____ Period: _____

Semester: _____ Date: _____

Concerns:

_____

_____

_____

_____

_____

_____

Arnold, H. *Succeeding in the Secondary Classroom.* © 2001. Corwin Press, Inc.

Awards and Certificates

Awards or certificates that are prepared by the teacher and given to the students are another positive method of communication with the parents (see Form 7.9). They show that you appreciate their children, and parents will often show *their* support of your classroom by their work as volunteers or for a special program, project, or event.

Mom and Dad Come to School

Preparing for a Parent Conference

Parents want to meet the new teacher, and this is an opportunity for you to learn about your students' interests, hobbies, talents, and any special health or medical needs. Parents are interested in what happens during the school day.

Invite your students' parents in for a conference. If there are issues that you need to discuss or clarify, don't wait for the district-scheduled parent conference week. Also, an open house is not the time to have a quality parent-teacher conference. Take the following steps when planning for the first parent-teacher conference:

1. Relax.

2. Set up a specific location and time.

3. Invite the parents to have a seat in your classroom.

4. Involve the parents in finding a solution for the problem.

5. Ask the parents if there is a history of the problem. If so, what can you do that is different?

6. Have your class records handy to refer to during the conference.

7. Show the parents any papers, homework, or projects that might assist in providing a solution to the problem.

8. Agree on a plan of action.

9. Arrange a future meeting to gauge the progress of the situation.

10. Stay calm.

FORM 7.9. Sample Certificate of Appreciation:
Homework Assignments

CERTIFICATE OF APPRECIATION

This certificate of appreciation is presented to

_____

for completing all of the homework assignments
for the first quarter of the fall semester.
Homework assignments were submitted on time to the teacher.

_____   _____
Teacher   Date

_____
Principal

_____
School

_____
Subject

The Conference

Parents want to work with the teacher, and to have an effective first-time conference, keep in mind that the conference must be planned for and should reflect organization and preparation.

The level of trust can increase between the parents and teacher if there is a willingness to work cooperatively to obtain a solution for the child. An understanding of your classroom, and the students while they are in your class, can provide for a much improved system of communication.

Keep in mind that, when the conference is arranged and confirmed, you need time to listen. The teacher should plan to listen to the parents to learn more about the parents and their children. Don't rush! Plan for parental input regarding the situation. When you meet, make sure that no other staff members are present so that the parents recognize that this conference is important.

In closing, think about your scheduling and timelines for a parent conference. Make sure that you are on time and that you are not running over, which can make the parents feel like their work is not significant.

After the Conference

After completion of the parent-teacher conference, plan to do the following:

1. Review your notes from the conference.

2. Contact the student and invite him or her to clarify issues related to the conference.

3. Share your knowledge of the situation and the parent conference with colleagues who may have a need to know about the situation.

4. Make contact with the parents after the conference. This might include the class newsletter, telephone calls, follow-up notes, and/or letters.

5. Schedule a follow-up session to review progress.

Finding Balance

Loneliness at the Chalkboard

The first year of teaching in a secondary school requires the ability to constantly shift gears. You will be confronted with issues of student learning, mastery, demographics, parents, politics, instruction, and curricular issues in addition to issues about working with colleagues and administrators.

You will need to work with students at their level of readiness but be aware of the need to change lanes. Time will be spent preparing for a lesson that might fail after the first 15 minutes. No one in your preservice program may have taught you about the numerous potholes that seem to appear out of nowhere. Teaching is a hands-on job!

School Politics

During the first month of school, you will meet with administrators, your mentor teacher, colleagues, parents, students, resource teachers, business leaders, and district office personnel. When you meet with school stakeholders, plan to ask questions about the school and clarify concerns that you have about the district and school policies. In many instances, there are backgrounds on certain issues so plan to listen so that you are aware of the concerns (complete Form 8.1).

Department Politics

You will find that there are politics along department and interdepartmental lines in the secondary school. Listen to the discussions and concerns of your colleagues and pay close attention to nonverbal clues at meetings so that you are able to ascertain the circumstances present in your department (complete Form 8.1).

Parent Issues

Communication with parents is important during the first month of school, and it is important that you have verbal interaction. A face-to-face meeting with parents during open house or a parent conference will assist in increasing the level of trust between parents and the teacher.

If there is an issue, contact the parents by telephone regarding the concern. By making contact at the initial stage of a problem, you are providing an opportunity for the parents to be a part of the solution. It is an opportunity to willingly work together with parents to provide an understanding of your expectations, goals, and procedures and to clarify an issue or concern related to their child (complete Form 8.2).

School Changes in the Middle of the Semester

Just when you thought you had received all of your classroom supplies, textbooks, and supplemental materials, you learn that there will be changes in the master schedule and that you will receive additional students on Monday! You may realize that you don't have enough

FORM 8.1. Sample Reflections on Politics Forms

Reflections

School politics:

_____

_____

_____

_____

_____

_____

_____

_____

Reflections

Department politics:

_____

_____

_____

_____

_____

_____

_____

_____

FORM 8.2. Sample Reflections on Issues and Changes Forms

Reflections

Parent Issues:

_____

_____

_____

_____

_____

_____

_____

Reflections

School Changes in the Middle of the Semester:

_____

_____

_____

_____

_____

_____

_____

classroom supplies, and you may feel emotionally unprepared for additional students. What do you do now?

The first month of school is filled with student program changes. This is your first teaching position, so be prepared to change some of the areas that you had meticulously planned for the semester (complete Form 8.2).

Student Politics

You have always wanted to be a student adviser for a school club. One of your administrators meets with you and asks you to become the adviser for a student club that will not take up too much of your time. After all, you are a first-year teacher and you want to become a part of the school community. What better way to get to know your students outside of the classroom?

Become a faculty adviser for a club. It is only takes a few hours each month, and you will receive monthly stipends from the school. Becoming a faculty advisor for a club is an opportunity to earn extra money and become acquainted with your students outside of the classroom. It is also an opportunity to share your love of an avocation with adolescents.

However, maybe not all of the students in the club are best friends (complete Form 8.3). How do you know? What do you do when you realize that there are student politics in the group that are having an effect on your classroom? What do you do? How do you recognize when there are some issues that are crossing over from the extracurricular, after-school club to your classes?

Answer the following questions to determine if you are ready to cope with student and school politics:

1. Can I (or will I) distinguish between conflicts of ideas and conflicts of personality?

2. Can I (or will I) refrain from sarcasm and cynical remarks?

3. Can I (or will I) refrain from being perceived as aggressive during conflicts?

4. Can I (or will I) hold back outbursts of my temper?

5. Can I (or will I) learn what my colleagues think of me?

6. Can I (or will I) see how I am perceived by my colleagues?

7. Can I (or will I) enlist the support of other new teachers?

FORM 8.3. Sample Reflections on Student Politics Form

Reflections

Student Politics:

_____

_____

_____

_____

_____

_____

_____

_____

8. Can I (or will I) enlist the support of members of my department?

9. Can I (or will I) work cooperatively with the school administration?

10. Can I (or will I) support the clerical and paraprofessional staff?

11. Can I (or will I) avoid past histories of differences coloring the present and future?

12. Can I (or will I) value others' opinions even though they are the opposite of mine?

13. Can I (or will I) not undermine the professional dignity of veteran teachers?

14. Can I (or will I) note what I have been asked to do and share with a colleague for assistance when checking for perception?

15. Can I (or will I) develop short-term and long-term action plans to assist in dealing with difficult situations?

16. Can I (or will I) cover myself?

17. Can I (or will I) not take everything that is said and done as personal?

If you are feeling lonely at the chalkboard, ask yourself the following questions:

1. Can I (or will I) visit my next door neighbor?

2. Can I (or will I) collaborate with another new teacher on a project, lesson, or field trip (see Form 8.4)?

3. Can I (or will I) keep my department chair informed?

4. Can I (or will I) keep my mentor teacher informed?

5. Can I (or will I) share teaching ideas with members of my department?

6. Can I (or will I) ask for assistance with materials and/or teaching strategies (see Form 8.5)?

7. Can I (or will I) clarify concerns and issues with others?

8. Can I (or will I) plan an activity and implement the idea?

9. Can I (or will I) enjoy a social opportunity with a colleague?

10. Can I (or will I) keep my eyes and ears open to new opportunities?

11. Can I (or will I) keep deadlines?

12. Can I (or will I) share my skills and interests with others?

13. Can I (or will I) promote the spirit of collaboration?

14. Can I (or will I) take the time to get to know others?

15. Can I (or will I) leave my classroom and meet others?

Evaluation

During your first year of teaching, you will experience successes and weaknesses. An administrator, principal, or vice-principal will be assigned to you for the purpose of evaluation. Each school district has its own system and forms of evaluation.

Following are some areas that you should consider as you think about your evaluation for the academic year:

1. Attend the district professional development meetings so that you understand the processes, procedures, timelines, and expectations.

2. Read all of the materials so that your responsibilities are clear.

3. Define your goals and objectives (see Form 8.6).

4. Make time to review the evaluation process with your school site administrator and the assigned district office administrator.

5. Clarify the observations and conference processes with your evaluator.

6. Learn the timelines associated with evaluation.

7. Review remediation plan options including timelines, procedures, and pertinent materials.

8. Confirm final dates for evaluation and review.

9. Create a professional development growth plan.

10. Update yourself on continued employment options.

FORM 8.4. Sample Colleague Ideas Form

Colleague Ideas

Date	Colleague	Curriculum Idea

Arnold, H. *Succeeding in the Secondary Classroom.* © 2001. Corwin Press, Inc.

FORM 8.5. Sample Colleague Resources Form

Colleague Resources

Date	Colleague	Resource/Materials

FORM 8.6. Sample Teaching Checklist

Teaching Checklist

- [ ] 1. How do I keep my students involved for an entire semester?
- [ ] 2. What does student success look like in my classroom?
- [ ] 3. Do all of my students know what is expected of them?
- [ ] 4. Is my classroom organized?
- [ ] 5. Are my students on task?
- [ ] 6. What do I do about student disruptions during the class?
- [ ] 7. What do I do if my students are confused about a lesson?
- [ ] 8. Is my classroom climate relaxed?
- [ ] 9. Is my classroom well managed?
- [ ] 10. What are my relationships with students and parents like?
- [ ] 11. Is my discipline policy clear and understandable?
- [ ] 12. Are my daily procedures and routine clear to students?
- [ ] 13. Is the physical arrangement of my class conducive to learning?
- [ ] 14. When do I set aside time for my lesson planning?
- [ ] 15. When can I meet with my mentor teacher?
- [ ] 16. Do I understand my recordkeeping procedures and processes?
- [ ] 17. How do I give class assessment feedback to my students' parents?
- [ ] 18. How do I build self-esteem activities in my class on a daily basis?
- [ ] 19. Am I realistic about my goals and objectives?
- [ ] 20. Do I value my students and parents? How do they know?

Professional Organizations

As a new teacher in your school district, you will be approached to become a member of your local educational organization (see Resource A). The decision to join your local professional association or union is personal. Your association is made up of teachers who are involved in negotiating contracts or agreements with the local school board.

At your new-teacher orientation, you will be provided with specific information regarding membership in the association. In your new-teacher orientation packet, some schools might include information and necessary paperwork for joining the association. The local union in the school district may also belong to a state and national organization. Teachers in your department, your mentor teacher, or other support providers can provide you with information regarding services, fees, benefits, and history.

General and Subject-Specific Professional Organizations

Your knowledge base of your subject area can be enhanced by joining an educational professional organization. It might be useful to obtain information from a variety of organizations, especially if you are involved in an interdisciplinary program in your school.

For those content-specific areas, a listing of some of the organizations can be found in Resource B. Following are two additional useful organizations that might be of general interest:

1. International Reading Association, 800 Barksdale Road, Newark, DE 19714

2. Association for Supervision and Curriculum Development, 1703 N. Beauregard Street, Alexandria, VA 22311-1714

Professional Development Growth Plan

Career development is a lifelong process. You have probably heard this in many of your preservice classes at the university. It is now in your hands and not for anyone else. You are now responsible for your career planning.

The induction year of teaching is the first teaching job and you are beginning a new cycle in your life. You have joined a school district, which is a large organization and includes a personnel or human resources department. Read the information from this department and get to know a person who might answer your questions and concerns regarding professional development growth plans.

In some school districts, it is the responsibility of the teacher in cooperation with an administrator to develop a plan. Other districts may have specific forms and procedures related to professional development. The personnel or human resources staff can assist you in clarifying issues regarding the timelines, procedures, and processes that are used by the district.

Speak with your principal and a staff member of the human resources department and learn what is required in your state and district to renew your teaching certificate. Do not wait until 3 months before the expiration date to take classes or workshops. The faculty lounge and your mailbox will be filled with announcements regarding courses, workshops, seminars, and international programs that might be useful to you in planning your professional growth. Some districts have a partnership with local colleges and universities that provide courses within the district at a specific school. These courses are often held after school or on Saturdays and do not necessitate your leaving the district to meet the requirements of certification.

There are several colleges that offer weekend courses, distance learning, and televised courses so that you do not have to leave the comfort of your home. Do not put off learning about the requirements that may affect your certification. Take some time and set up long-range goals for your particular needs. Your interests and needs play important parts in planning for your professional growth. Meet with your mentor teacher, department chair, or administrator to discuss your long-range goals and how they relate to your professional development.

Just as when you sat in your classroom and visualized what it might look like before the students arrived, think about yourself and your future. Where is it that you wish to go and how do you plan to get there?

In Closing

This book is designed to be useful for beginning teachers in middle and high schools. There are sound and practical ideas to assist the classroom teacher during the first months of school. This book is primarily written for those teachers who are new to teaching at the secondary level. Although those who work with younger children may find elements of the book helpful, it should be modified to meet the specific needs of the grade or subject area.

This book should be used as secondary teachers see fit; it is not meant to be read as a textbook. The teaching ideas in this book have come from secondary teachers who have been involved in a secondary beginning program. The book is designed to be a supplement, providing strategies and ideas while on the teaching journey.

The first months of school are challenging and exciting, and for the students and the new teacher, it will be the first time that they meet. Unfortunately, the first-year teacher will not have a second chance to make a good first impression. If you are a first-year teacher, your first impression to a group of adolescents sitting in front of you can be crucial to your success during the academic year. It is important that you make the best of this new situation.

The first weeks of school are the most productive and will reap many rewards to you as a beginning teacher. Spend the time to prepare, reflect, plan, and manage your classroom and it will be a more successful year for you. The students will grow, learn, and change during the year, and there will be opportunities for you to do the same.

To all of the new teachers, I wish you the very best first year of teaching. There are many teaching challenges that are before you at this time in your career.

"Whatever you can do or dream you can do, begin it!
Boldness has power, magic, and genius in it."

—Goethe

Resource A

Professional Organizations

American Alliance for Health, Physical Education, Recreation and Dance, 1900 Association Drive, Reston, VA 22091

Association for Childhood Education International, 4615 Wisconsin Avenue, Washington, DC 22016

Association for Computers in Mathematics and Science Teaching, P.O. Box 4455, Austin, TX 78765

Association for Supervision and Curriculum Development, 1703 N. Beauregard Street, Alexandria, VA 22311-1714

Council for Exceptional Children, 1920 Association Drive, Reston, VA 22091

Council for Library Resources, One Dupont Circle, Washington, DC 20096

Council on Teaching Foreign Languages, Six Executive Plaza, Yonkers, NY 10701

International Reading Association, 800 Barksdale Road, Newark, DE 19711

Music Educators National Conference, 1902 Association Drive, Reston, VA 22091

National Board for Professional Teaching Standards, 1900 M Street North, Suite 210, Washington, DC 20036

Phi Delta Kappa, English Street and Union Avenue, Bloomington, IN 47401

National Art Education Association, 1916 Association Drive, Reston, VA 22091

National Association of Biology Teachers, 11250 Roger Bacon Drive, Reston, VA 22091

National Association for the Education of Young Children, 1834 Connecticut Avenue NW, Washington, DC 20009

National Science Teachers Association, 1742 Connecticut Avenue NW, Washington, DC 20009

Resource B

Subject-Specific Organizations

American Alliance for Health, Physical Education, Recreation and Dance (AAHPERD), 1900 Association Drive, Reston, VA 22091

American Vocational Association (AVA), 1410 King Street, Alexandria, VA 22314-2749

Council for Exceptional Children (CEC), 1920 Association Drive, Reston, VA 22091

International Reading Association (IRA), 800 Barksdale Road, Newark, DE 19711

International Society for Technology in Education (ISTE), University of Oregon, 1787 Agate Street, Eugene, OR 97403-1923

Music Teachers National Association, 2113 Carew Tower, Cincinnati, OH 45202

National Art Education Association (NAEA), 1916 Association Drive, Reston, VA 22091

National Association for Gifted Children, 4175 Lowell Road, Suite 140, Circle Pines, MN 55014-3500

National Association of Geology Teachers, P.O. Box 368, Lawrence, KS 66044

National Business Education Association (NBEA), 1914 Association Drive, Reston, VA 22091-1596

National Council for the Social Studies (NCSS), 3501 Newark Street NW, Washington, DC 20016

National Council of Teachers of English (NCTE), 1111 Kenyon Road, Urbana, IL 61801

National Council of Teachers of Mathematics, 1906 Association Drive, Reston, VA 22091

Index

CORWIN PRESS

The Corwin Press logo—a raven striding across an open book—represents the happy union of courage and learning. We are a professional-level publisher of books and journals for K–12 educators, and we are committed to creating and providing resources that embody these qualities. Corwin's motto is "Success for All Learners."